Spotted Dolphins

ABDO
Publishing Company

A Buddy Book

by

Julie Murray

VISIT US AT
www.abdopub.com

Published by Buddy Books, an imprint of ABDO Publishing Company, 4940 Viking Drive, Suite 622, Edina, Minnesota 55435.

Printed in the United States.

Edited by: Christy DeVillier
Contributing Editors: Matt Ray, Michael P. Goecke
Graphic Design: Maria Hosley
Image Research: Deborah Coldiron
Cover Photograph: Minden Pictures
Interior Photographs: Corel, Digital Stock, Minden, NOAA (National Oceanic & Atmosphereic Adiministration), Photodisc

Library of Congress Cataloging-in-Publication Data

Murray, Julie, 1969-
Spotted dolphins/Julie Murray.
p. cm. — (Animal kingdom)
Summary: Introduces the physical characteristics, behavior, and habitat of spotted dolphins.
ISBN 1-57765-707-1
1. Stenella—Juvenile literature. [1. Spotted dolphins. 2. Dolphins.] I. Title. II. Animal kingdom (Edina, Minn.)

QL737.C432 M87 2002
599.53'4—dc21

2001053444

Contents

Sea Mammals

Dolphins, whales, and porpoises live in the sea. But these animals are not fish. They are sea **mammals**. Walruses, sea lions, and seals are sea mammals, too.

Mammals use lungs to breathe air. Mammals are born alive instead of hatching from eggs. Baby mammals drink their mother's milk. Giraffes, pigs, hamsters, and people are mammals, too.

Dolphins

There are 32 kinds of dolphins. They live in most oceans of the world. These sea **mammals** are very playful. They often leap out of the water. Dolphins will swim alongside boats, too.

There are many kinds of dolphins.

What They Look Like

The spotted dolphin is named after the spots on its skin. Light-colored spots are on its dark-gray back. Dark-colored spots are on its light-gray belly.

Spotted dolphins can grow between six and eight feet (1.8 and 2.4 m) long. They weigh about 250 pounds (113 kg). That is not much bigger than a person.

Spotted dolphins are named after their spots.

The spotted dolphin has a long, beak-like nose. It has a tall fin on its back. **Flippers** and a strong tail help dolphins swim. All dolphins have a **blowhole** for taking in air. This blowhole is on top of the dolphin's head.

The dolphin's big forehead
is called a melon.
Melon

Where They Live

Spotted dolphins live in the Atlantic, Pacific, and Indian Oceans. Some of them live far away from land. Some spotted dolphins live near the coast. The Gulf of Mexico has a lot of spotted dolphins. Some visit the coast of Japan, too.

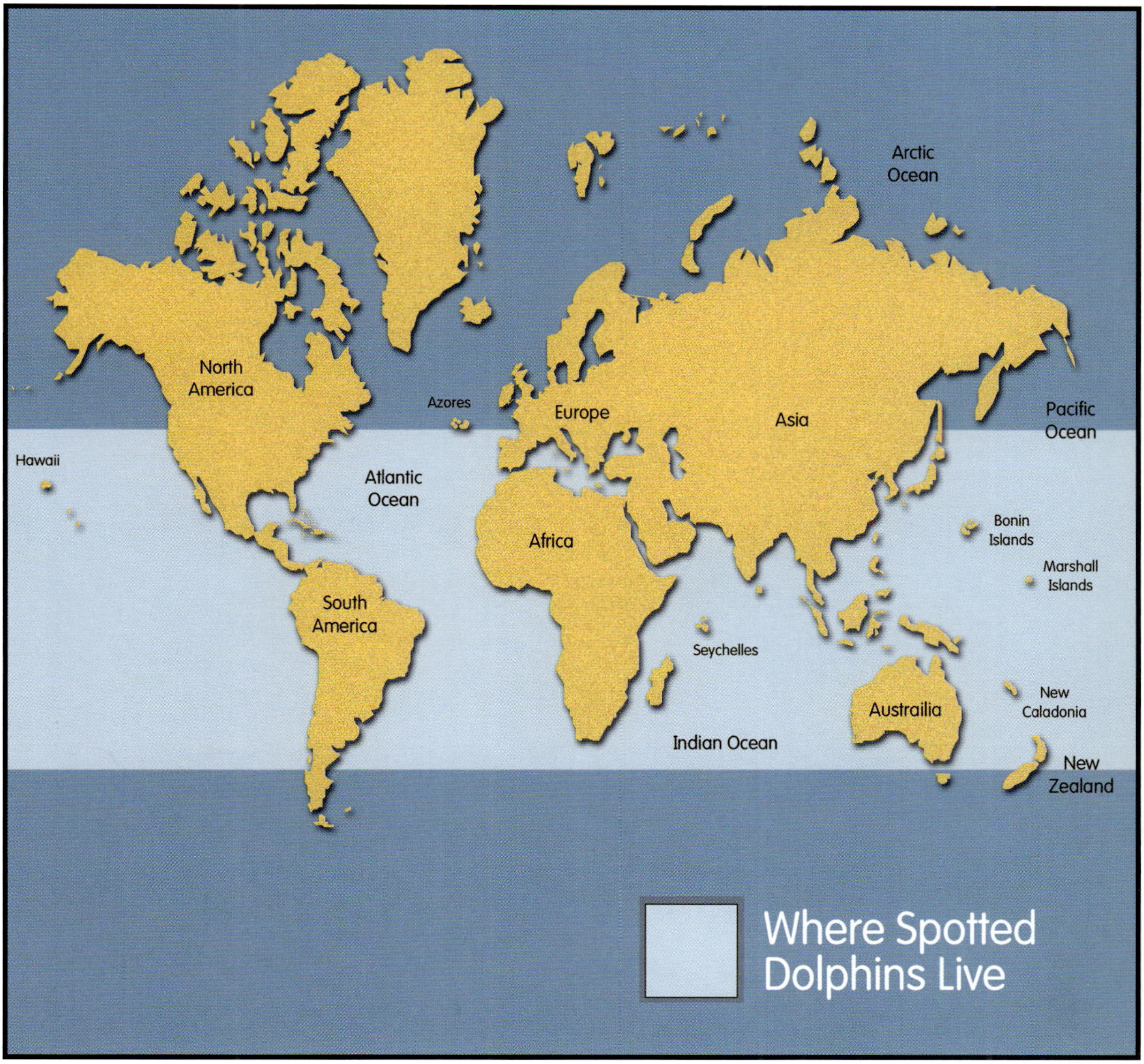
Arctic Ocean
North America
Azores
Europe
Asia
Pacific Ocean
Hawaii
Atlantic Ocean
Bonin Islands
Africa
Marshall Islands
South America
Seychelles
New Caladonia
Austrailia
Indian Ocean
New Zealand
Where Spotted Dolphins Live

Pod Life

Spotted dolphins like to be around each other. They live in groups, or **pods**. A pod can have as many as 100 members.

Swimming in a group helps spotted dolphins guard against **predators**. Some predators of dolphins are killer whales and sharks.

Spotted dolphins swim together in pods.

Eating

Spotted dolphins eat small fish and squid. Sometimes, a **pod** of dolphins works together to trap fish. They will swim underneath and around a **school** of fish. This makes it easier for the pod to catch fish. A dolphin catches a fish in its teeth. Then, it swallows the fish whole.

Some fish swim together in large schools.

Dolphin Sounds

Spotted dolphins use movements and sounds to **communicate** with each other. Dolphins make sounds like whistles, clicks, and chirps. Nobody fully understands what these dolphin sounds mean.

Dolphins also use sounds to find food. They will make a sound, then listen to the echoes. The echoes tell them the size and shape of what is ahead. This is called **echolocation**.

Echolocation helps dolphins find fish to eat.

Spotted Dolphin Calves

Female spotted dolphins have one baby at a time. Dolphin babies are called calves. Calves are born under water. Newborn calves are over two feet (61 cm) long. They do not have spots yet.

A spotted dolphin calf stays near its mother.

Newborn calves can swim right away. They drink their mother's milk. Six-month-old calves will start eating fish. A calf's spots may begin to show after one year. Calves may stay with their mothers for five years or more.

Important Words

blowhole the opening on a dolphin's head that is used for breathing.

communicate to give and receive information. Talking is one way people communicate.

echolocation using sounds and echoes to learn the shape and size of objects ahead.

flippers the flat, paddle-shaped body parts that dolphins use for swimming.

mammal most living things that belong to this special group have hair, give birth to live babies, and make milk to feed their babies.

pod a group of dolphins.

predator an animal that hunts and eats other animals.

school a group of fish swimming together.

Web Sites

Dolphin Anatomy

http://users.aber.ac.uk/als9/anatomy.htm
Read more about fins and other body parts of the dolphin.

Jaap's Marine Mammal Pages

http://ourworld.compuserve.com/homepages/jaap/cet-delp.htm
This web page features facts on different kinds of dolphins.

theBIGzoo.com

www.thebigzoo.com/Animals/Atlantic_Spotted_Dolphin.asp
Learn more about the Atlantic spotted dolphin.

Index